THE POWER OF QUESTIONS

HOW THE RIGHT QUESTIONS CAN LEAD YOU TO SUCCESS IN BUSINESS AND LIFE.

Ray Titus

DEDICATION

This book is dedicated to all the young employees of United Franchise Group and every student that has attended the Titus Franchise Center at Palm Beach Atlantic University since its inception. My dream is that all of you will learn the power of questions and never be afraid to ask questions. The more you ask, the more you learn. You also move ahead of everyone else who is either too timid to ask or has an ego that won't let them ask. Being a "know-it-all" is no way to go through life. In the old days, people would say, "Fake it till you make it", but that doesn't work long-term. Eventually, the truth will come out and you will learn that faking it is what frauds do. You want to be authentic and successful. You are much better off learning the right ways while you're young. Questions unlock all the answers in life, so...ask away! Don't worry about what others think about your questions or you. Asking questions will lead you to the answers that will unlock the full potential of your life.

Ray Titus

CONTENTS

Introduction 1

1. Sales 3
2. Interviewing For A Job 5
3. Negotiations 7
4. Managing People 9
5. Embracing Change 11
6. Dating 13
7. Church Hopping 15
8. Raising Positive Kids 17
9. Picking A School 19
10. Kids Spell Love: T-I-M-E 21
11. Lifelong Learning 23
12. Who To Ask? 25
13. Questions Are Compliments In Disguise 27
14. Life After Death 29
15. Your Legacy 31

Closing 33

My List Of Questions 35

Ray Titus

INTRODUCTION

We live in a world where people want to tell and show you everything they do. Social media has given a microphone and camera to everyone to share anything. Everybody wants to talk about themselves and show that they are leading a special life, but learning how to use questions to your advantage and benefit can be the key to everything, and these questions will lead you to a truly special life. The key ingredient is the ability to ask questions (not telling people things), especially well-thought-out questions that can take you to another level as a businessperson, spouse, parent, really with anything. We call it "peeling the onion". As you ask the second and third questions, it gets you much deeper into the true answer. As you uncover some very important information that makes it easier to make the right decisions, you learn that asking questions is the most important part of your journey to success in life.

The power of questions is unlimited potential if used properly and this short book will help you uncover the right questions to ask in many important areas of life; from the business side with sales, management, negotiating, to the personal side of dating, raising kids, and lifelong learning. The book ends with the biggest, most important question of them all…so sit back and enjoy this book. I have one question for you before you start, do you know what is stopping you from improving your life right now? "The Power of Questions" will help you answer that question and many others!

SALES

Most people think sales is talking and telling people about their products and services. True professional salespeople know that sales are about finding out what the customer wants and delivering it. How do you find out what they truly want or need? You need to get to know these future customers by asking questions like, "Where are you originally from?", "Tell me about you and your family." Getting to know the prospect better than you know the products and services is so important to getting very good at sales. You should be looking for connectors, these are things you may have in common with them. Sometimes, the customer doesn't even know what they want and may have an issue that they need solved. The quickest and best way to uncover it all is by asking questions. Probing questions like, "Ideally, what is it that you really want here?", or "Where do you see the biggest problem with this?". The questions are the first key to helping you uncover what they want. The second key is the ability to listen to them. So, asking questions and listening will lead you down the path to the sale. I know you may be saying "It's great going down the path, but how do I close the deal?", the answer is: you've guessed it! Questions! "What's stopping you from doing this right now?" is a question that has helped many salespeople close the deal much faster, "What can we do to make this happen now?" is another one. Many salespeople are afraid to ask questions for fear of losing the deal. This is a natural, but bizarre thought process if you really think about it because if you uncover the issues and challenges, and if you are a good salesperson, then you can get over every one of them! Many salespeople lose orders and they don't even know why. They are afraid to ask "Why?". They've already lost the order, the least they should do is learn why they lost it. Call the prospects that have not bought from you and find out why. Ask them probing questions that go deeper than "Was it something I said?" will help you improve as a salesperson more than anything else. Ask them, "What could I have done differently?", "Why did you buy it from them?", and "Could you give me some advice that would help me in the future?". So, again, sales are not about talking and telling people about your product or service but asking probing questions and listening to what they say, which will lead you to the sale. You should then custom-tailor your presentation to fit their needs and wants. By asking questions you can uncover the future issues that may lead to losing the sale and address them all. This is truly the proactive sales approach that is needed today.

INTERVIEWING FOR A JOB

Most people go into a job interview thinking about what their answers should be, and some of that is important. Understanding the job, the company, and what they are looking for must be considered. You need to do research before you go into any interview. You should also be thinking about what questions you can ask during the interview, but most importantly at the end. Doing some research means coming in with a copy of their website with notes on it and asking about the company, staff, and anything interesting on the website. Ask them good, probing questions throughout the interview and certainly at the end, like:

- "If I were selected for this position, what does success look like?"
- "Does the company believe in promoting from within?"
- "Are there seminars or any special training offered?"
- "What do you think I would need to do right away?"
- "How would I spend my time each day?"
- "What's the culture like here?"
- "How financially strong is the company?"
- "What happened to the person who had this position before?"
- "What makes you different from (insert competitor)?"
- "Who would I report to if I was hired?"

I would not suggest that you ask all these questions, just the ones that make sense at the time, but not having any, or worse, only having questions about pay and benefits is terrible. Think about how your questions will tell the interviewer what you care about. By asking the right questions you show the interviewer that you are very interested in the company and position. It shows them you care about doing a great job for them. After interviewing thousands of people over the last 38 years, I can assure you that you will stand out if you ask the right questions during an interview and you will have a much better chance of getting the job.

3. NEGOTIATIONS

Good negotiations are about asking the right questions. Questions that uncover key points will help you negotiate the best deal possible. What if there was one question that you could ask that would help you save money in most negotiations? Would you ask it? It's as simple as asking: "Is that the best price you can do for me?", then just look them in the eyes and wait for them to give you a better deal. You hardly ever get something if you don't ask. The old saying goes, "Everything is negotiable." and it's almost always the case. "If I bought this today, would you throw in xx?" is another question that can help you get more for your purchase. Sometimes, a good way to start with people is to ask them if they had a blank piece of paper, what would a good deal look like? In other words, "Ideally, what do you want?". Sometimes you need to write down where you stand and put your offer next to what they are asking. Visualizing it can help lead you to an answer. Compromise used to be considered a good thing, but today it is viewed as bad. I don't agree, I think it can and should be viewed as a positive step toward getting something done. Almost everything in life is a negotiation to some degree. From small things like where you eat, what movie you watch, where you go on vacation, to buying a car or house, they all come from good or bad negotiations. You also must be willing to walk away from some deals. I guess my questions for you are: How important is this transaction to you?, Do the pros far outweigh the cons?, and Have you put together a scorecard to see the pros and cons? More questions lead to more insight into the other party's position which will lead you to closure either way. There is an interesting thought process for answering someone that goes like this: Feel, Felt, Found. "I understand how you feel, I felt the same way, until I found out about this new way or equipment." This is the empathy the prospect is looking for if you can't just say yes. Lastly, you must learn that "no" is not always a bad word. It's not as easy as just saying yes, but it is not always bad. Saying "No, I'm sorry, I can't agree to that." makes things much clearer to the other party and makes it real. Normally, you can't just be a "yes" person and make a good, fair deal, like it or not. "No" is a part of the negotiation process.

MANAGING PEOPLE

Learning how to manage each person takes time because you don't manage everyone the same way. You should never treat everyone the same, but treat them all fairly. Think about it, how could you treat an employee who has been with you for 25 years the same as someone who you just hired? Like everything in life, respect must be earned over time. The key to getting to know how to manage them is asking them questions. Where are you from? What motivates you more, money or an award in front of your peers? Have you played on a sports team before? Which sport and what was your position? How many brothers and sisters do you have? Are you the oldest, middle, or youngest sibling? All these questions, and many others, will help you better understand the employee. Next, get to know the employees in different settings by taking them to breakfast or lunch or meet their significant other at a corporate function. Getting to know the employees and what they value most will help you understand what motivates them and why they do the things they do. When employees bring you their issues or challenges, do you just bark out the answer? A better way is to ask them a simple question that makes them think. It also trains them to always come to you with a solution for the issue or challenge. The simple question is: "What do you think you should do?". You need to train them to think up solutions if you ever want them to stop coming to you for every answer. Simple rule, if they come to you with a problem, they must have at least one solution! Don't accept it when they say "I don't know.", say back to them, "Well, think about it and get back to me." Make them think! You must challenge employees to think and improve themselves. Following up with employees and asking how it is going with (Fill in the project) shows them you care and are willing to help them get it done.

EMBRACING CHANGE

Recently, I was asked what is the single most important characteristic or skill I look for when hiring people, and I answered, "The ability to embrace change." Give me a good, hardworking employee with a positive attitude that accepts change quickly and easily, and I'll show you an "A" player. There is probably no more important area to get good at asking questions then when we experience change of any kind. "Why do we need this change?", "How will this change make things better?", "How much training will I need?", "Where can I get help as we go through this change?". These questions, and many others need to be asked so you can get comfortable with the change. The world continues to change faster and faster and we must stay up to date or become extinct. When I first started to work, I was very enthusiastic and had lots of questions. I would ask why we do things a certain way and the answer I received most was, "because that's the way we have always done it." I refused to accept this answer. This answer teaches you nothing. There is always a better way to do something and we should always be looking for it. Often people fight change, especially with technology, and it's usually because they don't want to take the time to learn a new way. I read an article that said every individual that doesn't embrace AI and ChatGPT will ultimately get replaced by AI and ChatGPT! Embrace the new technologies and look for ways that they will make you and your business better and more productive. The question most people ask is, "Why do I have to do this?", the answer is that the time to change is before you must! Embracing change is the only way forward. Do you really think that you can just keep doing things the way you always have and be successful if everything around you is changing? Embracing change is critical to your future, and asking questions about any changes will help you accept them much faster and make it easier for you. If you are the employee or business owner that accepts change without complaints, but with a list of questions, you will inevitably be the more successful person.

DATING

Probably the biggest decision any of us make, besides choosing Jesus, is in choosing our future wife, husband, or significant other. We will spend more time with this person than any other. How do we decide? The first thing that we all start off with is, "Am I attracted to this person?". Disposition and personality do matter, but you must be attracted to each other to start off. Next, I believe that finding someone that brings out the best in you is critical. Is the other person positive or negative? Do they make me laugh? Are they fun to be around? After that, it comes down to getting to know the other person's wants, needs, and dreams. Do they match yours? You need to ask them a lot of questions. Ask about their goals, how they were raised, their family, and ask about what they are looking for in a spouse. There are many ways marriages can go wrong, cheating being #1, but religion, money, and sex seem to be the other biggest reasons. You need to ask probing questions about these very important subjects and many others. Some of this will feel uncomfortable but you are better off asking now than having problems later. I have seen just as many people fall "out of love" as I have seen them fall in love. Why? Sparks flew and they misinterpreted infatuation for love. Love is something you grow into after the sparks fly and you really get to know each other. My mother-in-law always says, "If there is a problem, it always starts in the bedroom.", and she's 86 years old! Sex is very important to all humans and you need to be on the same page. You always hear about money issues leading to problems or the affair that ruined a marriage, but being on the same page with religion is just as important. If you are going to raise children together, what is your shared belief going to be? Let's go back to money. Are they a saver or a spender? Do they believe in sacrificing things today for a better future? Are their credit card bills already too high? Dating can be a lot of fun, but as you get more serious with the other person, you must ask a lot of questions. Many Christians only believe in intentional dating, which is to only date someone that you may marry. How would you know unless you go on dates and compare? Getting to really know what you like and don't like is critical during this time, so go on dates with many different people and go to dinner, to the movies, to lunch, for coffee, but don't do anything other than ask questions and figure out who is right for you. These experiences will help you figure out what and who you are really searching for. If you haven't found that special person yet, don't get frustrated, get focused and go where they might be. Some great places to go where you may just bump into someone are the gym, church, Whole Foods, and work. Go early to all of them or stay late. You never know who you may meet!

CHURCH HOPPING

My wife and I were both raised Catholic and were married in the Catholic Church, but when we moved to Florida it became apparent that we needed to go to a different church. There were just too many things we didn't agree with in the Catholic Church. Manmade doctrines that were not even in The Bible. There were also times in my life where it was confusing as well. Let me give you an example of one. When my sister got married, she married a man that had been divorced. He did not get married in a church so the Catholic Church did not recognize his marriage, but they recognized his divorce and wouldn't let he and my sister get married in church. Seems very hypocritical to me. My wife and I started asking each other questions like, is this where we want to raise our kids? Do we have the same belief that we were raised with? Will our kids go to church if we stay here? Do we enjoy coming here each week? At that point we decided to try some other churches. We started church hopping to find our church for our family's future. We almost stayed at the Methodist Church, but the pastor was single and had several girlfriends in the church. Not what we wanted for our boys. After many questions and visits, we decided on First Baptist Church, which has since become Family Church. We could not be happier with our choice. Each week we learn from The Bible, hear great music, and enjoy great fellowship. The church is led by our pastor, Jimmy Scroggins. Our family has embraced this church and often we all sit together and go to breakfast at my favorite place, Surfside on Palm Beach. We will talk about the sermon and get into the message. If we never asked questions or just stayed where we were out of habit, we would never have reached this great point in our lives. Thank God for questions and Family Church!

RAISING POSITIVE KIDS

Kids are natural question askers as they are curious about how things work. Kids will constantly ask questions, that is unless they are "trained" not to. If they are made fun of or they are found at fault for asking questions, they will stop. "Why do you ask so many questions?" is a terrible thing to say to anyone, especially kids. Kids must learn that questions are not a sign of ignorance, but a sign of true intelligence. When I came home for dinner each night I would ask my kids the same question, "What was the best thing that happened to you today?". It would force them to think from the positive side each day. If you ask them, "Did you have a good day?" they can answer yes or no without elaborating. Making your children think of the best things that happen each day pushes them to focus on the positives instead of always thinking about the worst things. Positive thinkers lead the world, while negative thinkers become victims and we all know that victims never win. As we become adults, many of us stop asking questions and become "know-it-alls". The adults that keep their curiosity and keep asking questions are the more successful people. Elon Musk is one of the most curious individuals, and it has led him to incredible success. When someone says "why?" you should respond with "why not?". Just because something worked in 1960, 1980, or 2000, doesn't mean it will work in 2024! Be willing to learn from today's parents, but on the other side, the young parents of 2024 could learn a lot from experienced parents if they would just ask them questions. "What did you find worked best?" or "How did you get us to do that?". A great side benefit to raising kids is all the lifelong friendships that we have gotten through their school, sports, and church! Next step…raising positive grandchildren!

PICKING A SCHOOL

We could be talking about when parents need to pick a grade school for their children, or when high schoolers need to look at colleges. It is very important to put time into picking the right school either way. With either one, there are questions that need to be asked, but before I get to them, let's talk about who to ask. I remember my wife and I visiting grade schools together to find our first son AJ's school. We visited so many schools and spoke to the principals and presidents, it was a frustrating and difficult process. When we told my dad about it, he said "Why would you talk with the principal, president, or even the teachers? Go talk to the janitors, they will know what's really going on at the school and they will be honest with you." What great advice. We asked the janitors: "What type of kids were at this school?", "Are there drugs here?", "Would you send your kids here?". It was eye-opening how straightforward and honest their answers were, and it helped. Here are some other questions to ask everyone else, "What is this school known for?" "What's the best part of being at this school?" "What would you change about this school?" You should be aware of everyone and everything you see at the school. Ask questions on the tour and see if the students respect the tour guide or authority. Are they respectful of visitors? Making a list of all the things you want in a school and comparing each of the schools is a great way to come to the right decision.

KIDS SPELL LOVE: T-I-M-E

When Andrea and I decided to have children, we also decided we were going to work at being the best parents possible. We read books, spoke to our parents (asking them questions), and went to a seminar. The seminar was by Josh McDowell, and one of the things that resonated with us was when he said, "kids spell 'love' T-I-M-E." No matter how good a parent we could become, we knew we would put in the time with our children so we would be successful! Putting in time meant volunteering at school, going to church together as a family, eating dinner together each night, and basically always being there for them. We also got to know their friends very well, and yes, through asking them questions we learned who would be good for them and who wouldn't. "What is it like at home?", "Who do you look up to?", "What are your favorite things to do?". There was this time when one of our sons decided that he wanted this kid to be his friend. This other boy was very strange and while we were proud that our son would reach out to him, we were also concerned. There is a difference between missionary work and building up your friend group. Not too long after, our son decided he didn't have a lot in common and moved on, but this only happened after we asked him a lot of questions like, "What do you have in common with this kid?", "Do you think he's going to be a good friend?". Steering kids down the right path is part of a parent's job, not making every decision for them, but "steering" them. Never stop asking them questions to help them uncover the right path. Don't just tell them, show them by asking the right questions, they will see it for themselves. I know parents today that have kids that are 25, 30, and older and they are still heavily involved in all their decisions. How is that good training for when they are gone? It's not, and they need to let go.

LIFELONG LEARNING

I've found the most incredible way to live is to always be positive about life. As Zig Ziglar always said, "Be a good finder." Look for good in everyone and every circumstance. Always be positive about every circumstance and you will find the right path. The best way to become more positive is to become a lifelong learner. When you become a lifelong learner, two things happen: you learn a lot and get the answers you need, and you look at life differently – you're always looking to improve so you become more positive overall. I'm a huge believer in reading books because they have led me to incredible success in life. How do you find the right books to read? Often, I will be reading a book or a magazine article and they mention another book that the author received some great ideas from. I always write the name of the book down and later add it to my library. Some great questions to ask others are, "What's the best book you've ever read?", "What book has had the greatest impact on you and your business?", "What book have you learned the most from?" Once you get the answers, it's as easy as just buying those books and reading them! Then of course, to accomplish anything, you must take 3-4 good points from each book and apply them in your life. Today you can also ask about podcasts and TED Talks that have had the biggest and best influence on them. Who is the best speaker to listen to? All of them help you become better and more successful in life. Always look for the "silver lining" in every bad situation you find yourself in. Remember that positive people lead and win in every area of life while negative people lose. Becoming a lifelong learner and committing to always looking to improve changed my life, and it can change yours at any age. Today I read over 40 books a year and write one. I have been doing that for seven years as this is my eighth book. It is never too late to join the lifelong learners club.

WHO TO ASK?

Okay, so say you agree that asking questions is the key to accomplishing so many things in life, but now you want to know who to ask. The right questions to the wrong people can lead to disastrous results, right? No, this is only true if you do it the same way. You certainly don't want to follow their mistakes, but you could learn from them! Throughout life, you must be in search of who to ask questions of. Who do you respect and why? What do you want to accomplish? Who has already done it that you are close to? Is there an expert in this area that I can call? You probably know someone who knows someone who could be your biggest asset. You would be shocked at how many great people will answer your questions and help you even though they have no idea who you are! There is an old story about Steve Jobs calling one of the founders of Hewlett-Packard, Bill Hewlett, directly out of the telephone book (remember when we had a telephone book?), he had questions for him and ultimately got a job there years later! What is so special about this? He was 12 years old, and he had the guts to call the founder of a huge company. Obviously, this experience helped him later in life, but simply because he asked great questions at such a young age, it impressed an entrepreneur who ended up hiring him. I will often read a book or an article and then email the author about it. You would be surprised how many people respond. It's as simple as looking for and finding successful people, and then asking them questions to help you accomplish whatever you're looking to accomplish. There are a lot more good people out there than there are bad ones, so ask away! If you do run into a jerk who won't help you, move on to the next person.

QUESTIONS ARE COMPLIMENTS IN DISGUISE

What does this mean? When you ask someone a question, it tells the other person several things:

1. You are interested in what they are saying.

2. You are interested in learning more.

3. You are willing to learn from them!

The right questions are truly compliments. If we all could embrace this philosophy and encourage it within our employees, spouses, and kids, we would see huge improvement in relationships, your business, and our society. What stops us from asking questions? Mostly it's our ego as we get older. We don't want to look dumb, so we don't ask questions. By not asking questions, it ensures that you will stay uninformed in this area. The more uninformed you become, the more likely it is that you will make mistakes and fail. Ask questions, become smarter, it's that simple. When you ask questions, always have a pen and pad and take notes. It's a compliment to take notes when others speak, and you will be able to refer to those notes forever. Think of it as your personal diary for success! The bigger that book gets, the more likely it will be that you will experience success. So, we are back to asking questions, and then really listening to the answers.

LIFE AFTER DEATH

I would guess that the number one question for humanity over time is and always has been, "What happens when we die?". If you were to die today, are you certain you would go to Heaven? This is the question most pastors ask, and should, as it leads people to think, and maybe even change their ways. For many people, this question dictates how they live and act. People that do not believe in an afterlife tend to live for today, they seem to be more cynical about life, and certainly about religion and church. Faith is what comes into play here; do you believe in Heaven and Hell? This and many other questions about the afterlife are normal and healthy questions. They should be asked to your Pastor, Priest, Rabbi, etc., and you must start to get your mind wrapped around what your belief is. I choose to believe in Jesus and Christianity. You may see things differently and choose a different path, but to me, believing in Jesus and all he did for us has helped me accept death and look forward to the afterlife. I am not afraid of death because I know I am going to a better place. While I believe strongly in my faith, it does not mean that I never have questions. My pastor believes questions are good and not a sign of unbelief. We don't all have the answers nor understand it all. That's why they call it "faith", but being curious is good, so keep asking questions until you get yourself in a spot where you accept a religion or belief. My prayer for you is to believe in Jesus because my faith says that if you believe in Jesus you will go to Heaven. It is not based on good deeds; it's based on your belief that Jesus Christ is our savior and he came into this world to die for our sins. My questions for you are "If it's true, wouldn't it be a great thing?" and "If it isn't, don't you end up in the same place you are right now anyway?". I believe it's true.

YOUR LEGACY

While this entire book has been about questions you should ask in different circumstances, I wanted to ask you a question, "What will your legacy be?". In other words, what will you be remembered for? You shouldn't wait until the end of your life to think about your legacy. You should be proactive with it and work toward what you want. Mine will be family and business, or to put it better "family business". We have a great business with a lot of family members involved. We have given to many charities and started the Titus Center for Franchising at Palm Beach Atlantic University. This is the first school in a University for Franchising. Franchising is what we do best. However, I would really say my business is about family. It started with my wife, Andrea, who was introduced to me by my father at work, and continues with our three boys, AJ, Austin, and Andrew, Laura and Allie, our daughters-in-law, Abigail and Hannon, our granddaughters, and my sister Ellen and her three boys, Brady, Shane, and Dustin. All six boys are full-time in the business. I will be passing the business onto the next generation, and in the meantime, not only making the company bigger and better, but training them all to take it to the next level when I'm gone. We also have many employees who have been with us for 10, 20, and 30 years who are part of the family. Today we have 15 second-generation employees, so yes, we are a family business to the extreme. Many of our franchisees have passed their business to the next generation, others have built great businesses and sold them to have more money for retirement. Either way, we should be looking to live a life of significance. What will your legacy be? Don't wait, and don't live life without working toward the legacy you want to leave behind.

CLOSING

In closing, I hope that by reading this short book you have learned some good questions to ask to help you improve and be more successful in many different areas of life. Think about it, with any failures you've had in life up to this point, if you had just asked the right person the right questions before it, you probably wouldn't have failed. Most importantly, I hope that you come away from this book agreeing that asking questions is a sign of intelligence. Don't let your ego stop you from asking questions. Become a lifelong learner and stay curious of everything in life. Don't be afraid to ask anyone any questions. Remember that questions are compliments! May God bless you in the future. I have one question for you... Do you now have five or more questions that will help you live a better life?

Also, you now know the answer to my first question in this book. "What is stopping you from improving?" Obviously, the answer is you if you aren't asking enough questions. My prayer is that no matter how old or young you are, you have decided and committed yourself to becoming a lifelong learner and to improve and get better for the rest of your life. Thank you for reading this book, now please pass it on to someone else that could use it.

💡 MY LIST OF QUESTIONS 💡

1. _____

2. _____

3. _____

4. _____

5. _____

6. _____

7. _____

8. _____

9. _____

10. _____

Made in the USA
Columbia, SC
18 June 2024